Helping the Lost Pets Home

By Cameron Macintosh

Mike and Gem were playing with Gem's dog, Dutch.

Gem's dad showed them his phone.

"The Lost Pets Home has posted a note online," he called. "It says the home must close!"

Oh no!
We adopted Dutch from there!

“We should raise some cash to save the Lost Pets Home!” said Mike.

Dad suggested that they wash bikes for people.

Gem and Mike rushed out to set up.
Mike filled a bucket with soapy water.

SAVE THE LOST
PETS HOME

Soon, Pip and Hank were rolling their bikes to the stall.

"Would you wash my bike?" Pip asked.

"Yes!" said Gem.

“My wheel needs to be fixed,” called Hank. “Can you do that?”

“Yes, we can!” Mike said.

Tran wheeled her bike up to Mike and Gem.

"Do you want some help washing the bikes?" asked Tran. "Then you could wash even **more** bikes!"

"Great!" shouted Mike.

Tran parked her bike, and Gem handed her a bucket.

The stall got busy!
Soon, a long line of bikes was filling the street.

Mike, Gem and Tran brushed, mended and washed many bikes!

Mike was spraying the hose.

Gem was lifting the bikes and fixing the wheels.

Tran was cleaning mud off the bikes.

People waited in line and then added some coins to the jar.

“We collected so many coins!” yelled Gem.

“Thanks for helping us, Tran!” said Mike.

No problem!
SAVE THE LOST
PETS HOME

“I hope we helped the Lost Pets Home, Dutch!” sighed Gem.

Dutch was feeling very happy!

CHECKING FOR MEANING

1. Where did Gem get her dog, Dutch, from? *(Literal)*
2. Who helped Gem and Mike wash all the bikes? *(Literal)*
3. Why do you think Gem and Mike wanted to raise money for the Lost Pets Home? *(Inferential)*
4. How do you think the manager of the Lost Pets Home will feel about the kids' donation? *(Evaluative)*

EXTENDING VOCABULARY

wheeled	The word *wheeled* is an example of a verb that is made out of a noun. What noun is it made from? How does knowing the noun help you understand the meaning of the verb *wheeled*?
mended	Which word in the text has a similar meaning to *mended*? What kinds of things might you mend?
spraying	What is the base of the word *spraying*? What is the difference between spraying water and tipping water?

MOVING BEYOND THE TEXT

1. Gem and Mike raised money to donate to an organisation that was special to them. What are some ways that you could help an organisation that is special to you? How might you help around your school?
2. Why is it important to wear a helmet and other safety gear when riding a bike?
3. How do you think the Lost Pets Home helps animals and their owners?
4. What are some ways that people can try to find their pets if they are lost?

TIME TO WRITE

Write about what the Lost Pets Home might do with the money that Gem and Mike donate.